# IMAGES OF W

# THE FRENCH ARMY IN THE GREAT WAR

## RARE PHOTOGRAPHS FROM WARTIME ARCHIVES

### David Bilton

Pen & Sword
**MILITARY**

First published in Great Britain in 2019 by
**PEN & SWORD MILITARY**
An imprint of Pen & Sword Books Ltd
Yorkshire – Philadelphia

ISBN 978-1-47388-724-4

Typeset by Concept, Huddersfield, West Yorkshire, HD4 5JL.
Printed and bound in India by Replika Press Pvt. Ltd.

Pen & Sword Books Ltd incorporates the imprints of Aviation, Atlas, Family History, Fiction,
Maritime, Military, Discovery, Politics, History, Archaeology, Select, Wharncliffe Local History,
Wharncliffe True Crime, Military Classics, Wharncliffe Transport, Leo Cooper, The Praetorian Press,
Remember When, White Owl, Seaforth Publishing and Frontline Publishing.

For a complete list of Pen & Sword titles please contact
PEN & SWORD BOOKS LTD
47 Church Street, Barnsley, South Yorkshire, S70 2AS, England
E-mail: enquiries@pen-and-sword.co.uk
Website: www.pen-and-sword.co.uk
or
PEN & SWORD BOOKS
1950 Lawrence Rd, Havertown, PA 19083, USA
E-mail: uspen-and-sword@casematepublishers.com
Website: www.penandswordbooks.com

# Contents

Introduction . . . . . . . . . . . . . . . . . . . . . . . . . . . . . . . .    5

Background . . . . . . . . . . . . . . . . . . . . . . . . . . . . . . . .    6

The French Army at War  . . . . . . . . . . . . . . . . . . . .   11

Bibliography . . . . . . . . . . . . . . . . . . . . . . . . . . . . . . .222

# Introduction

The subject of the French army in the First World War is vast, far too vast, to cover in a book of this size. The illustrations herein help tell of some of the battles fought and some of the changes that took place during the conflict. It is not possible to deal with any battle in detail; there are other books which do that. However, the French army has been sadly under-examined by English historians.

I have provided a general history of the main events of the war on the Western Front, the main theatre of French activity, but have also included some photos taken on other fronts: the French also fought in Africa and in Italy, Salonika and in the Dardanelles. There is no attempt to analyse or place it in the context of other aspects of the war; the text focuses on the French story in France and Belgium.

Any mistakes are solely my responsibility.

## Acknowledgments

Once again many thanks to Anne Coulson for reading the draft and to The Prince Consort's Library for giving me access to their books.

# Background

T he evolution of the army that fought in 1914 began in 1868 after the unsuccessful campaign in Mexico on behalf of the Emperor Maximilian. Before that, the army had fought successfully for almost thirty years, in North Africa, the Crimea and northern Italy. The failed Mexican campaign, coupled with the knowledge that the Prussian army numbered around 1,200,000 men (including reserve), meant not only a restructuring but also an increase in manpower was necessary. As a result, although opposed by both the Right and the Left political wings, compulsory military service was introduced. Senior officers favoured a professional army undiluted by conscripts, and the future draftees, mostly factory and farm workers, objected to being forced to join the army.

This was all too late to prevent defeat during the Franco-Prussian war. By this time the army had increased in number from 288,000 to 393,000, but many were spread across Mexico, Algeria and Rome. After reserves had been called up it amounted to 567,000, but this was still less than half the strength of the combined German states. The disparity in numbers was made worse by a defective mobilisation process in which men were often called up to units some distance away. After a long journey the men would arrive to find their units had mobilised without them.

In Paris, left without a government (which had moved to Bordeaux during the fighting), the National Guard and a provisional municipal government – known as the Commune – took over. With the return of the French government to Versailles, fighting broke out between released prisoners of war and the Communards. Little quarter was given during the fighting; vicious savagery besmirched Paris, the City of Light. It is estimated that government forces killed between 20,000 and 25,000 men and women.

With the suppression of the Commune, the rebuilding of the army began. Defeat brought the realisation that a stronger army was necessary to fight Germany again, either to repel further invasion or regain the lost provinces. The army became more popular with the middle and upper classes, while the working classes accepted their military obligation.

Many young and ambitious officers feared that if they served abroad they would miss the next war, and would be at a disadvantage when war did start. However, those who had done colonial service where they were engaged on active service had not only gained valuable fighting experience, but also won decorations and distinction.

This resurgence in popularity was short lived. Two sensational affairs involving the army did considerable damage to its status. The first involved Général Boulanger, who, having appeared to be on the point of leading a right-wing coup, fled to Brussels and there committed suicide on his mistress's grave.

More damaging still was the Dreyfus affair. This, a conspiracy against an innocent Jewish artillery officer, 'caused a great revulsion of feeling against the army when the truth became known'. The revulsion destroyed the perpetrators and also many who had no connection with the conspiracy, shattering public confidence in the army. However, despite an anti-militarist spirit amongst intellectuals, and leaders of the Left, the strengthening of the army continued.

These affairs had a profound effect on the officer corps. The number of applicants for officer training at Saint-Cyr dropped and many career artillery and engineer officers resigned. The absence of quality applicants was soon felt in the École supérieure de la guerre, which supplied men for the general staff, and this undermined the quality of the officer corps in the early years of the twentieth century.

Nevertheless, efforts were made to increase manpower. By 1893 this had been achieved: the French and German armies were almost at comparable strengths. Initially it was envisaged that the army would be used to defend France along specific lines and at fortifications at Épinal, Toul and Verdun. However, by 1889 it was decided that, when war came, the army would go over to the offensive, leading to attacks on Metz and Strasbourg – Plan 10.

When it was discovered that the German birth rate was growing quicker than the French, an alliance with Russia was formed to further boost the number of men who would be available to fight the Germans, and 'national service was fixed at three years for all'. For some reason national service was cut to two years in 1905, reverting to three years only in 1913. This last 'change gave France more men under arms in peace-time than Germany' although Germany was more populous.

Changing the length of service had an unintended consequence: a lack of quality NCOs. Many of the best were commissioned – before the war half the officers had come from the ranks – others found administrative positions. Others not so able left after fifteen years' service to become minor civil servants. Although two years' national service was sufficient time to train a soldier, the third year had given them time to develop into NCOs. As a result, the army's tactical efficiency was reduced.

Added to the Metropolitan troops were those from the colonies, a further 90,000 men, both European and native, many known for their picturesque uniforms. Included among the colonial troops were the men of the Foreign Legion, volunteers from around the world and troops from Africa and Indochina. At the start of the war 'there were twenty-one battalions of Senegalese in Northern and Western Africa, as well as ten battalions of Malagasies and one of Somalis; two regiments of Congolese in Equatorial Africa; and five Indochinese Regiments.' Five battalions of Senegalese troops in North Africa were sent to France at the beginning of hostilities. Many other new Senegalese battalions were raised for overseas service during the war. Most of the Indochinese and Malagasy troops served at depots, although some did see combat. 'In all, the empire produced 600,000 soldiers for the war effort and sent 184,000 workers to French industry.'

The use and employment of these colonial men was governed by racial stereo-typing. 'Indochinese troops, though intelligent, were assigned almost exclusively to armaments and aviation factories; the Hovas of Madagascar were sent to the ambulance corps, but also to the artillery; North African and Senegalese infantry were thrown into almost all of the major offensives, but even Mangin (a colonial soldier) divided his black troops into "warrior races" – those from the savannah – and the rest, who were employed as workers or replacements.' There was an element of mistrust. While North Africans fought in their own regiments, black troops fought as battalions interspersed with white troops until the final offensives of 1918.

With the outbreak of war, foreign volunteers for the French army were placed in the Foreign Legion. Heavy losses and the return of men to their own armies forced a reorganisation of the four wartime regiments into the *Régiment de Marche de la Légion Étrangère,* a unit that won many laurels. German and Austrian volunteers were retained for action in Morocco and the Sahara.

During a period of considerable military innovation, senior French officers came to the conclusion that the next war would be won by the development of the offensive spirit. They believed that the French soldier 'lacked the ability to stand on the defensive under a prolonged storm of fire'. *Attaque à outrance* – to excess – became the official doctrine. Jerram, in *The Armies of the World,* wrote in 1899 that 'Drills, manoeuvres and military instruction generally are founded on the principle that the offensive alone permits of decisive results.' This was to lead to the deaths of thousands during the battles of the frontiers in August 1914. With an attack being met with massed rifle and machine gun fire, a soldier was summed up as having 'two chances of life and one of being killed' with virtually no chance of surviving without a wound.

By 1900 the strength of the army 'totalled 27,450 officers and 517,000 men. The war establishment, which included the reserve of the active army, the territorial army and its reserve, could call upon approximately 4,660,000 men of all ranks, of whom about 500,000 were untrained.' To maintain this level of manpower, service was compulsory between the ages of 25 and 45, with three years in the active army, ten in the army reserve, 'and six years each in the territorial army and reserve'. The war strength of the active army reserve was approximately 1,300,000 men while the territorials had a total strength of 2,270,000. Their role was primarily static defence at fortified positions and on lines of communication. The main fighting was to be done by the active army and its reserves.

The yearly intake of men, around 230,000 plus volunteers, was dealt with on a district basis, with France being divided into eighteen military districts. Algeria comprised an overseas district, the 19th. Each district comprised a recruiting depot and mobilisation cadres which were allocated to an army corps of the same number as the district. In turn each corps comprised two divisions and a brigade of cavalry. By 1914 there were twenty-four districts and corps.

Infantry in the active army was organised into eighteen regional regiments, with thirty battalions of *chasseurs à pied* and four regiments of light infantry, with 145 sub-divisional regiments, each of four battalions. Further battalions were provided by the *Infanterie Légère d'Afrique*, whose personnel 'were either men released from military prisons awaiting the end of their engagement, or petty criminals convicted in France. Discipline in these units was at least as tough as in the Foreign Legion.

There were eighty-nine regiments of cavalry: thirteen Cuirassiers, thirty-one Dragoons, twenty-one Chasseurs, fourteen Hussars, six *Chasseurs d'Afrique*, and four Spahi – light cavalry recruited from the native population of Algeria. Each regiment consisted of five squadrons, four active and one reserve and, at war establishment, consisted of five officers and 155 other ranks. The artillery was formed into forty field and horse regiments grouped into nineteen brigades of two regiments with two unassigned. Each brigade was attached to an army corps with one regiment assigned to the corps, the other to divisional use. 'There were also a further eighteen fortress artillery battalions' plus mountain artillery and independent *groupes* in Africa.

The structure of the territorial army was similar, with '145 infantry regiments, seven battalions of *chasseurs à pied*, ten battalions of Zouaves, 150 squadrons of cavalry, nineteen regiments of artillery, and eighteen battalions of engineers.'

Active service units were closely supported, as in every army, by a range of other personnel. 'The Administration embraced not only clerks and General Staff, but also supply troops and medical orderlies.' Traffic was controlled in rear areas by *Commissions Régulatrices Automobiles*; movement of materials was under the *Train des équipages*, and the *Service Automobile*, formed from the *Train*, provided drivers for staff cars and trucks. 'The *Service de Santé* was the medical branch, and consisted in one of two specialities – doctors or chemists (orderlies and stretcher bearers were provided by the Administration branch or by individual units).'

As the war progressed, trench mortars were formed and manned by artillerymen, and in late 1916 a tank arm was formed as part of the artillery. 'Towards the end of the war, a number of French army units were formed from prisoners of war and from volunteers transferred from the *Legion Étrangère*, and these went on to form the nucleus of the armies of independent Czechoslovakia and Poland.'

Although the *Service Aéronatique* was formed in 1903 as an engineer unit, by 1912 it had become a separate organisation. Although still within the army, it is outside the remit of this book which will concentrate purely on the land-based forces.

At the start of the war, therefore, France could field an army comparable to Germany but only in the short-term. As a nation, she could only produce 60 per cent of the potential manpower of Germany. Although this could be partially addressed by the use of colonial forces, that solution raised political and military difficulties. While colonial troops proved effective in the attack and during good weather, many were not up to the demands of trench warfare in the cold of northern France and were unsuited to the static nature of the war after November 1914. This did not stop their employment in the Dardanelles or on the Western Front until mid-1917. 'During the Nivelle offensive of 1917, their casualty rates were catastrophic – two or three times that of white units – and not surprisingly, some of the black units broke and ran. After this, most of the black troops were withdrawn from the front lines and the high command dropped any ideas of further large-scale use.'

Alone among the major powers, France had not adopted any form of camouflaged uniform for use in Europe, in contrast to some colonial troops who were wearing khaki-coloured clothing. The red trousers were little different from those worn eighty years earlier, as was the képi, and the dark blue tunic too added to the high visibility of the French soldier. At the start of the war a new uniform was on trial: a light blue – horizon blue – cloth (that provided no camouflage) was selected and went into production at the end of August 1914. It was some time before complete uniforms were to be available. As a stop-gap, dark-blue over-trousers were issued from October 1914, which were worn on their own when the weather was warm. Some infantry were issued with fire brigade blue trousers; others received corduroy in brown or dark blue. Eventually uniformity was achieved, with the only distinguishing feature being the collar patches and trouser piping. The uniformity was only among Metropolitan troops; units from overseas were generally wearing a shade of khaki from 1916. Some colonial regiments had arrived in a yellower version of khaki which they continued to wear. The képi, although it continued to be worn by most officers, was replaced by a side cap.

A steel helmet was authorised in early 1915 and officially adopted on 21 May. By 23 December 1915, over 3 million Adrian helmets had been produced, all identical except for the metal badge on the front. Initially painted in horizon blue, their colour was later changed to khaki.

# The French army at War

To cope with the shortage of men, it was essential that the war should be over quickly. The French army needed to take the offensive at all costs. The plan was simple 'but it was also obvious and surprisingly naïve, factors which are not good qualities in a military plan.' A system of huge fortresses along the border with Germany was designed to funnel the attacking force into a gap in the defences where they could be destroyed. Though such a plan lacked élan, it would be better for the army to attack the enemy armed with 'valour, a thirst for glory and revenge and the offensive spirit'. By the spring of 1914, Plan 17, an impressive piece of administrative planning that detailed the mobilisation and deployment of the army, was complete. What was lacking was the formal plan for an attack; that would be left until later.

The main aim would be to regain the lost provinces, even if this meant ignoring intelligence that the German attack would be through Belgium. To the French high command this meant the impassable Ardennes, which would allow the French left wing to cut the German attack in half. When the German attack came it was through the flat Flanders plain where there was little in the way of fortifications to slow the enemy down. As well as ignoring German intentions, they also ignored the possibility the Germans might use reserve troops to provide more men, something the French would not do in attack.

It was not a good start for the French army, especially as the German army moved most of its troops to the Western Front, leaving far fewer men to face the Russians. Facing the 1,071,000 French soldiers and 150,000 British were 1,485,000 Germans. Outnumbered and in highly visible uniforms, the French army would suffer over 500,000 casualties by the end of 1914. The high losses were made worse by as many as two thirds of infantry officers becoming casualties.

Importantly, the Germans were aware that the French would almost certainly attack in the Alsace/Lorraine region, a choice which suited German intentions well. As the French could not attack through Belgium until it was invaded, the decision was made to invade German territory which naturally included prepared defences. The terrain was difficult even for infantry, who could be directed by the defenders into areas that were better suited to defence; it was even more difficult for the supporting arms to follow up any successes or provide needed materials.

Ignoring intelligence reports, on 14 August 1914, Dubail's 1st and Castelnau's 2nd Armies began their offensive. The columns marched off-road, at snail's pace, and 'consequently neither army made more than a few miles in the first day.' It was not until the next day that the frontier was crossed which had been abandoned two weeks before for diplomatic reasons. German resistance was limited to isolated positions with the defenders leaving when the French appeared. With massive artillery superiority they were content to cover their retreat and harass the attackers.

Progress on 16 August was quicker, but topography was splitting the two armies apart. Eventually they lost contact, and even the use of cavalry to attempt liaison failed. With conflicting demands on manpower as the armies diverged, Joffre transferred a corps to Belgium. Fortunately the enemy kept withdrawing, but at the same time bombarded the French line of advance with heavy artillery beyond the reach of the French 75s.

The French advance looked impressive on the map, but the line was not secure and German resistance stiffened as they got closer to the gateway to the Rhine valley. It had been a ploy: unknown to the French, a counter-attack was being planned. It would be made easier by the transfer of another French corps to Belgium. The Germans now fielded nineteen against eleven French divisions.

Sarrebourg fell after fierce fighting on 20 August, but most German forces made little progress against determined resistance by Dubail's army. The same could not be said of de Castelnau's 2nd Army. They had come under unexpected attack in exposed un-entrenched positions. Wave upon wave of German troops poured down in converging columns from the surrounding forests, carrying all before them, with the exception of Foch's XX Corps. They repelled every attack and believed they were on the verge of victory when the order to withdraw arrived.

The withdrawal left the Bavarians miles behind and it was not until 25 August that German troops appeared on the Meurthe. During that time, Joffre had forbidden any further withdrawal and the French had organised a powerful front.

During that time, further north, the French began the battle of the Ardennes. It lasted just two days. After heavy rain on 21 August, followed by a heavy mist that became a fog in the morning, the French V Corps 'wandered into the German XIII Corps which was preparing to attack'. After two hours of battle the fog lifted, allowing the Germans to shell the 75s in close support of the French infantry, and to launch their own attack. The French V Corps withdrew, followed later in the day by VI Corps. While the two divisions of IV Corps held their ground and II Corps was able to assist IV Corps, the failure of the attack by the 3rd Colonial Division, at a cost of 11,000 casualties, allowed the Germans to disrupt any French plans.

The next day, elements of the Colonial Corps reached Neufchâteau without undue difficulty, although harassed by Uhlans and observed by planes. However, XIII Reserve Corps was waiting, with a force twice the size of the French attackers. Although they gave a good account of themselves they were forced to pull back to their start line during the night. Similarly the attack by XII and XVII Corps was stopped, with the latter corps giving brief resistance to a German counter-attack. One artillery unit left their guns to the enemy without a fight. The whole corps took flight and was not rallied until it was far behind its start line. It had been a disastrous day with two corps severely mauled, I Colonial and XVII, the latter also having been routed, while XI Corps was fought to a standstill.

Attacks planned for the next day went ahead. These again met with no success and the Fourth Army finished the day further to the rear. Shortly after midnight on 24 August, Joffre ordered the army to withdraw beyond the River Meuse. Although the French Third and Fourth armies had not been successful, they had not been broken and an important lesson had been learned. Joffre instructed that in future, before sending infantry in to capture a strongpoint, the attack should be 'prepared with artillery' and the infantry 'held back and not launched until the distance to be covered is so short that it is certain the objectives will be reached'.

Further north, the Fifth Army was holding positions in the south of Belgium. As the left wing of the French army, with the British on their left, they were facing the main German thrust. The fighting on 21 August resulted in German troops capturing bridgeheads over the River Sambre. Without permission, the next day, two corps 'launched their men through the morning mist into close and bloody conflict with the Prussians.' They blundered into their opponents unawares. 'By evening the whole French line had been driven back over 5 miles from the Sambre and by a force half their strength.' By 23 August, the enemy had driven the Fifth Army back to their starting positions, from where they 'launched a furious and successful counterattack'. This did not stop the German attackers, who by late afternoon had numerous crossings across the river. The next day, 'the great retreat had begun'.

The 1919 Michelin guide book described the next period of the war as a 'heroic retreat, without precedence in history, which attained a depth of 122 miles, and in the course of which the Allied soldiers, though already fatigued, marched as much as 30 miles a day facing about from time to time and counterattacking fiercely, often with success'.

A first line of resistance during the withdrawal was on the River Somme. Although it was heavily contested, it was realised that the battle front could not be reformed there successfully. Joffre ordered the withdrawal of the whole front towards Paris and the River Marne. On the same day as Général Gallieni, Military Governor of Paris, issued his proclamation stating his intent to defend Paris to the end, German cavalry patrols were sighted at Écouen just 8 miles from the city.

Instead of driving straight to Paris, the German forces changed direction. After heated discussions with Joffre, Gallieni ordered Sixth Army to attack, while at the same time the rest of the British and French forces withdrew.

The French attack resulted in a thirty mile gap in the German line. When the British moved north, and were reported to be moving into the gap, German plans had to be rethought. This, along with German intelligence misreading the situation in Belgium, where 3,000 British marines began a landing on the Belgian coast by Russian and British troops, and faltering attacks at other places along the front, resulted in the order for two German armies to fall back.

German troops halted their retreat along the line of the Aisne, in 'eminently defensible positions just north of the river'. The Miracle of the Marne now became the Battle of the Aisne.

The Germans now 'formed a strong defensive line from the Oise south of Noyon, along the high ground behind the Aisne to the Meuse north of Verdun, and to the south of Saint-Mihiel'. They had trained to create wire defences and trenches. A war of movement was becoming one of static defence systems, a type of warfare the French had ignored in their pre-war training. The French were also suffering from a shortage of ammunition which allowed the Germans to dig in more easily.

'Mid-September was to see the first example of the slogging infantry trench war-fare to come. Joffre ordered an attack by Maunoury's exhausted 6th Army, the BEF and, on the right, the 5th Army against the German positions on the steep, scrubby heights north of the Aisne and the Chemin des Dames.' In wind and rain, although badly coordinated, the attack was initially successful. However, the German defences proved too strong and the attacking infantry were mown down by well-positioned German machine guns on the heights.

French losses included two battalions that surrendered at Brimont; also a 'German counterattack at Courcy put the French defenders to flight'. The French were again on the defensive, losing Fort Brimont, but they successfully held onto Reims. 'Heavy fighting continued until 18 September with intermittent fighting further east until the 27th.'

To the east, in an area that would later become infamous for its horror, the Germans began their attacks on the defensive positions at Verdun. Attempting to turn the flank of the Third Army, they were stopped by artillery fire from the forts. The fort at Troyon fell after a five-day siege. Two weeks later, Camp des Romains, a fort between Toul and Verdun, was forced to surrender, creating the Saint-Mihiel salient.

With positions becoming entrenched in the centre and east, the Allies moved their armies northwards in an attempt to outflank the enemy, who were attempting to do the same to the Allies. After desperate fighting Arras was held, the Germans were checked at Hazebrouck and the line on the Lys reoccupied, but Lille surrendered.

Further north, the Germans managed to cross and hold a bridgehead on the Yser in spite of determined counter-attacks by a French territorial division. Fortunately, the large German attack round Ypres was held by British and French troops. Again the French army had suffered considerable losses. The Flanders fighting resulted in a casualty list of 50,000 killed, wounded, PoW or missing, while the estimate for the four months of the war was 300,000 killed, including many of the best officers.

# 1915

The New Year saw both sides sitting in trenches with little possibility of manoeuvre warfare. When the British and French halted the attack on Ypres, and the Germans had to send their reserves to Russia to help the Austrians, it took pressure off the French army and allowed them to reorganise and move units around to more appropriate positions.

However, there was no change in tactics, with Joffre continuing 'to believe that formal frontal attack, properly prepared and motivated, must achieve a break-through'. The story for the Allies in 1915 'is one of a series of fruitful attacks by both the French and the British that, at best and at heavy cost, only moved the opposing trench systems forward for short distances'.

Apart from the small sector held by the Belgians, and the British holding positions around Ypres and south, the French held most of the Allied line. Only three areas were found to be, at times, impracticable for fighting: the Flanders coast where artillery turned any ground not flooded in to a mire; 'artillery destruction among the Argonne hills and woods created almost impassable conditions' and the highlands of the Vosges were so unsuitable that both the French and the Germans used the area for recuperating troops, its normal garrison being low-grade men.

Joffre continued to focus his attention on the German salient pointing towards Paris. By attritional attacks in the Artois and Champagne regions he hoped to wear down German strength in order to mount a breakthrough offensive. The pattern of December's small-scale attacks along the whole front was continued in January; their purpose was to secure positions for artillery observation.

To British readers, the most famous area subject to such attacks was Vimy Ridge. Its capture, along with Notre Dame de Lorette, was essential to provide observation on the plains behind. Other areas included La Main de Massiges, Le Vieil Armand at Hartmannswillerkopf, Tahure, Soain and Vauquois. Such attacks were costly and not always successful, as shown in the eighteen assaults over a period of seven weeks: the French lost 20,000 killed or wounded at Éparges between Verdun and Saint-Mihiel.

The Germans were also mounting small-scale attacks to gain local superiority, such as the successful attack in January to take Hartmannswillerkopf. Three French counter-attacks in the summer regained some of the lost ground, but that was lost to a German counter-attack in October. The final French attack in December resulted in heavy casualties, especially among élite *chasseurs alpins* troops, for no gain.

Champagne saw the first large-scale attack. For a month the French 'made repeated attacks on the German strongpoint system over the bare Champagne hills,' advancing just 3,000 metres, at the cost of 40,000 casualties. In Saint-Mihiel a supporting attack also made little progress.

A month later the Germans launched an attack at the British front around Ypres. Although the British and Canadian troops bore the brunt of the attack and also most of the casualties, the French 45th and 87th Territorial divisions were involved. Affected by the German gas, 'several thousand men fled, terrified, gasping and retching,' but the number of casualties was relatively low. One battalion broke, murdering its officers, and both divisions, due to the speed of their retirement, lost their artillery. The day after the German offensive finished, a French attack succeeded in pushing the Germans back across the Yser canal.

On 9 May, a six-day bombardment between Arras and Lens marked the start of the next French offensive. The aim was to take Vimy Ridge, Notre Dame de Lorette, and advance to the River Scarpe. After bitter fighting, the French had advanced 4 kilometres, at a cost of 300,000 casualties, a third of them deaths. They had not captured the ridge.

The arrival of further British divisions released a French army for operations further south and, in the same period, expansion of the French army created twelve new divisions. Joffre used the situation to launch two simultaneous attacks in September: Artois and Champagne, with priority being given to the latter.

With bands, bugles and drums playing in the trenches, the Champagne offensive began. The French succeeded in breaking through the first line of defence, taking 14,000 prisoners, but, even though reserves were brought forward quickly, the German second line held. After a temporary halt to the offensive, fresh French attacks were met by fresh German reserves. Holding well-prepared fortifications and pillboxes, in a deep defence system that the French field guns could not neutralise, they took a heavy toll of the attackers who were mown down in their hundreds by machine gun and rifle fire. 'The same fate befell two cavalry divisions, the speed of the charge being powerless to prevent the horses and their gallant riders being massacred.'

In contrast, after just one day of the Artois offensive, Joffre ordered the attack to cease. Losses for the two battles, for minor gains, were 190,000 with 30,000 killed. However, the Champagne battles did not finish until 6 October, and, in Artois, there was a final unsuccessful attack on Vimy Ridge on 1 October. 'By the end of 1915 the French army had suffered 1.2 million casualties, including 350,000 killed or missing.'

# 1916

Once again, the arrival of fresh British divisions allowed the French to hand over a further part of the front. The French 10th Army on the Arras front was relieved early in the year and moved south. The plan for 1916 was a major, war-winning offensive in the early summer.

The situation changed on 21 February when the Germans attacked Verdun where the guns and garrison had been run down by Joffre to reinforce other more important sectors. In 1916 it was a dangerously exposed salient which the Germans could fire on from three sides.

Confirmation of the attack was provided by deserters and French intelligence with the primary target of Fort Douaumont being confirmed. The Germans also concealed their attacking troops by constructing underground galleries. Preoccupied with Somme preparations, removal of the guns defending Verdun continued. They were to be used on the Somme but some extra troops were sent to the area in compensation for the loss of guns.

When the assault was launched, the defending troops were of varying quality: two reserve divisions, a regular division and one from Algeria. While many were elderly territorials, the battalions also included Tirailleurs Algériens, Zouaves and élite *chasseurs à pied*. They faced 'some of the best and most battle-hardened divisions in the German Army.'

The attack was preceded by the most intensive artillery bombardment of the war so far. However, although the shelling had inflicted heavy casualties, the initial German probing attacks with flamethrowers were 'met with a spirited resistance and even small local counter-attacks in the best 1914 tradition from the battered French lines.' As a result, German gains were minimal.

After a further bombardment the next day, the German attack was more effective, pushing the French troops back. By 23 February, the two territorial divisions were almost spent, being replaced by the Algerian Division, which in turn was destroyed piecemeal and eventually broke. Général Chrétien's XXX Corps had virtually ceased to exist when the first units of the 'Iron Corps', Général Balfourier's XX Corps, arrived, having marched for two days through snowstorms without food, artillery or machine guns.

On 25 February, the Germans scored a major victory when a handful of men entered Fort Douaumont through an unguarded gun embrasure. Fortunately, effective French artillery fire helped prevent further German success.

Reinforcements in the form of Pétain's 2nd Army were then authorised, with the order that Verdun must be held; Général Castelnau had overall command of the area and gave Pétain the right bank to defend. With further troops and artillery arriving, clearly defined sectors were assigned to each unit, and more effective artillery fire on German positions and roads north of Douaumont resulted.

The problem of supply was efficiently solved by a conveyor belt system of some 3,500 lorries. Half brought up supplies, the other half returned with casualties or relieved troops. New troops marched on either side of the road down to the fortress. After the war, the small road became known as *la voie sacrée*. It was very efficient – in all weathers, mostly at night, it supplied 50,000 tons of supplies a week with, at peak periods, one vehicle every ten seconds. It was most important that the flow was maintained so that, if a vehicle broke down, it was simply pushed off the road.

Renewed German attacks on 6 March met a stabilised French front and determined resistance with counter-attacks; little ground was lost. A further attack on 14 March, which lasted a month, was fought over ground where the French trenches no longer existed. It met a similar fate: 'small local gains'. After the launch of yet another major attack on 9 April, little had changed by the end of heavy fighting in deep mud. However, by the end of May and another major assault, this time in a heat wave, the French had lost Mort Homme and Hill 304. Gains of up to 7 kilometres on the right bank were 'contained by effective French local counter-attacks.' In a campaign designed to bleed France white, German casualties were 120,000 and French 133,000.

At the end of April Pétain was relieved and replaced by Nivelle, a man who believed in the all-out offensive, assisted by Général Mangin, nicknamed 'the butcher' because of his indifference to loss of life. Their first attack was to retake Fort Douaumont; it was a costly failure.

The Germans were aware of Joffre's plans for an offensive on the Somme and opened a new attack on 1 June. On 7 June, Fort Vaux surrendered. This was followed by an assault on 23 June that pushed the French back 'to the perimeter defence of Fort Souville and the outer defences of Fort Tavannes', and forced the abandonment of Fort Thiaumont.

On 11 July, the final German assault, this time in the Souville area, met determined resistance and failed. With the Eastern Front needing men and the Somme taking priority for ammunition, German attacks stopped, to be replaced by French counter-attacks that continued into August.

The French now went over to the offensive. After a 300,000-shell barrage on a 5-kilometre front, French infantry advanced, supported by a creeping barrage on 24 October. Fort Douaumont fell, on 2 November Fort Vaux was taken, and by mid-December the French front was 5 kilometres in front of Douaumont. Verdun had been saved. 'The casualties in the eleven months of fighting amounted to 330,000 Germans, of whom 143,000 were dead or missing, and some 351,000 French losses, 56,000 dead, 100,000 missing or captured and 195,000 wounded.'

Such a massive effort at Verdun naturally reduced French participation in the Battle of the Somme. From an intended 40 divisions, only 16 would be available, of which just five would be involved on the first day.

Although the French army made a much smaller contribution, it was considerably more successful than its British ally. Starting slightly later, after a more devastating artillery preparation on a much smaller frontage, and assisted by a mist, XX Corps took the German first-line positions but could go no further due to lack of British success. South of the Somme, two divisions had overrun the German second line by the end of 3 July, holding the high ground overlooking Péronne; again limited British success halted the French advance.

In September, Général Micheler's 10th Army advanced 5 kilometres south of the Somme towards Chaulnes. North of the Somme, a French attack met with initial success but stalled due to a lack of available reserves. The assault was resumed in tandem with the British attack using tanks, but after two weeks of fighting only Combles had been taken. As autumn began, the French stopped their attacks. The Somme had cost the French 37,000 dead, 29,000 missing or prisoners and 130,000 wounded.

Joffre had made plans for 1917 but these were never to come to fruition. He was replaced by Nivelle and eventually retired as the first Marshal of the Third Republic.

# 1917

Apart from a minor action in January 1915, the area on the Chemin des Dames was a relatively quiet sector until mid-1917; quiet enough for units to be sent there to rest and reorganise. Facing the French was the German 7th Army, dubbed the *schlafende Heer* (the sleeping army). The area was to become the starting point of the French offensive under Général Nivelle. His intention was for the French troops to smash through the front in just 48 hours to the open country behind the front. Originally planned for the Somme, it was switched to the Aisne.

Scheduled in the first place for February, delays pushed the start to April and, with the German withdrawal, the plan had to be amended. The main offensive would be on the Aisne with a secondary attack east of Reims. To tie down German reserves, the British were to attack near Arras and the French *Groupe d'armées du Nord* at Saint-Quentin. These would be followed by the main thrust against the Chemin des Dames by the *Groupe d'armées de Reserve* and a day later by the attack east of Reims by the *Groupe d'armées du Centre*.

With revolution in Russia, and the entry of the United States into the war, there was discussion about whether the attack should be scaled back. It was not, even though the government was concerned about the potential scale of the casualties.

The unwanted attack had a further issue. The scale of the offensive was difficult to hide from the air and from the high ground held by the Germans. Added to this there were few guns capable of firing deep into the German defences, with a shortage of shells for all types of artillery, while poor weather and German air superiority made observation difficult.

Attacking on a 40-kilometre front, the aim was to pinch out the salient between Vailly and Moulin de Laffaux while also attacking towards Juvincourt. After further postponements the attack began on the morning of 16 April 1917. There was no breakthrough; the gains on the first day were no more than 1 or 2 kilometres deep. It was the first time that the French army had used tanks. Used as close support for the infantry, mobile artillery, they were not a success. Of 128 Schneider tanks, 52 were destroyed by German artillery and 28 broke down.

The next day the main effort was transferred to an attack north-east by 5th Army, while 6th Army continued its attack of the previous day. Although 5th Army failed to make progress because of bad weather, on 18 April the Germans pulled back from Vailly to the crest of the Chemin de Dames.

On 22 April, the offensive was switched to partial attacks for limited objectives. Their aim was to capture the plateau and push the Germans back from Reims. Ammunition shortages, coordinating four armies, and bad weather delayed the attacks, one of which was scaled down to limit casualties. The attacks were launched on separate days, 4th Army on 30 April, 5th Army on 4 May, and 6th and 10th Armies on 5 May. Again they were not the successes hoped for. At a heavy cost some tactical gains were made. The French *Official History* estimates losses of up to 134,000 killed, wounded or captured between 16 and 25 April.

Nivelle was replaced by Pétain but this did not stop 'the breakdown of discipline that now paralysed the French army. Disorders had started to break out on 29 April, and the scale of the crisis was unprecedented. Fortunately, the soldiers continued to hold the front; their grudge was against attacks where losses were unjustified by gains, not against defending France.'

Although the mutinies began during the offensive, the 'frequency and seriousness of the incidents actually increased after 15 May – after the offensive had been suspended and after Nivelle had been replaced by Pétain. Not until after the first of June did the crisis reach its peak.' Although the Germans were aware of a problem, they did not attack.

During this period, almost certainly reflecting the general war-weariness felt in France, many troops disobeyed orders. They formed assemblies, threatened their officers, demonstrated and refused to return to the trenches. Most of these were short-lived outbreaks; units correcting the backlog of overdue leave also helped reduce their severity. During this time, Pétain began his programme of modernisation while waiting for the arrival of the Americans. Much has been written about this period that provides a much clearer explanation of the problems than can be detailed here. 'The lasting effect of the mutinies, however, was that after them French commanders, formation and unit alike, had to include the morale factor as one of their most important considerations when planning all operations ... costly or large-scale offensives could no longer be mounted in the conditions of 1917.'

The mutiny was extremely serious and affected two-thirds of the French army, that is, 68 divisions from an army of 112; 44 divisions were unaffected. Of these just 5 were profoundly affected, 6 very seriously affected, 15 seriously affected, 25 affected by repeated incidents and 17 affected by just one incident. Most of the indiscipline came from the infantry regiments, the men who were complaining about attacks where the casualties were out of proportion to the gain. According to Pedronici, 'there were 250 cases of collective indiscipline. All took place in infantry regiments, apart from 12 in artillery regiments. In all, 121 infantry regiments, 23 battalions of light infantry (élite infantry), 7 regiments of colonial infantry, 1 regiment of territorial infantry (the oldest reservists) and 7 artillery regiments.' It is estimated that only 35,000 men, in approximately 250 cases, played a part in the mutinies out of an army of 3,500,000.

It is important to note that even though a division was affected, it did not mean all 15,000 men mutinied. It was often just a handful and they could be coerced back into the line given the right officers. Taking the example of indiscipline in the 20th Infantry Regiment, just 200 out of approximately 2,000 men mutinied on 29 April, while they were resting at Châlons-sur-Marne. 'They dispersed into the woods. The next morning, their regiment was sent back to the front without them. Most of them, appalled, re-joined it in time. Only fifteen faced trial, six were sentenced to death and none were executed.' A more serious incident in the 36th Division resulted in twelve soldiers and two corporals being court-martialled, five being sentenced to death. One was reprieved by President Poincaré, three were executed and one escaped just before his execution. One regiment, after two days of protest meetings and assemblies, returned to the front with cries of 'Down with the war!'

The most important mutiny occurred on 1 June at Ville en Tardenois and Chambrecy and involved two regiments of the 43rd Division. They demonstrated and paraded and sang the *Internationale*. Initially dispersed, they congregated again later in the day and assaulted their commanding officer. The next day the demonstration numbered 2,000. A quick solution to the problem was to bus the regiments to separate areas. Only once did men refuse to take further part in a battle in which they were already engaged. In most cases during the mutiny, even 'when considerable groups of soldiers belonging to several units of a division refused to obey, nearly all of them submitted after a few hours, leaving only a few dozen irreconcilables.'

Given a ratio of 1 mutineer in every 100 soldiers, it was obvious to the high command that most men were disciplined and could be relied upon. However, they still had grave concerns about the reliability of the divisions in reserve. If the Germans launched an assault, they would be needed at the front. Given the mutinies, the high command was worried about whether they would move to the front, and if they did, would they fight? Fortunately the Germans did not realise the seriousness of the situation, merely thinking it was a lull in the offensive. This gave Pétain time to attempt 'to heal rather than punish his army'.

There is no definitive account of the number of executions but it is thought that seven mutineers were shot summarily. 'There were forty-three certain executions (twenty-seven for collective indiscipline and sixteen for individual indiscipline).' There were far more non-capital sentences given to the mutineers. Of the 2,873 men convicted, heavy sentences of over five years' hard labour were given to 1,381 men and 629 were sentenced to death but their sentences were later reduced.

Although the offensive had finished, the positions of the two armies, both at the top of the plateau, meant that what had been a quiet sector could no longer be so. Fighting continued throughout the summer. 'At stake was a string of observation points that dominated the Aisne or Ailette valleys, such as Le Panthéon, La Royère, Froidmont, the *Monument* at Hurtebise, and the sugar-beet refinery at Cerny, and their names became notorious.'

With neither side strong enough to mount a major attack, attrition ground both sides down as a result of numerous local operations. The frequent German attacks recaptured some lost ground and were a good training ground for the new assault detachments, the *Stosstruppen* (shock troops).

The breakthrough occurred at the end of October when a French 'bite and hold' operation seized Fort de la Malmaison. With the loss of this position, the remaining German lines were enfiladed by French artillery, forcing them to abandon the entire length of the Chemin des Dames. French losses were relatively small with 2,241 killed, 8,162 wounded and 1,602 missing.

After the mutinies, Pétain adopted a defensive strategy with carefully prepared limited attacks that would 'bring success proportionate to the casualties ... and wear out the enemy.' However, he did commit the French to support the British offensive in Flanders. In the first assault, the 1st Army crossed the Yser canal with minimum casualties.

A limited offensive was launched at Verdun between 20 and 25 August on a 17-kilometre front: Hill 304 and Mort Homme were retaken.

# 1918

France's diminishing manpower resource was a major problem, with casualties averaging 40,000 a month and a requirement for over a million replacements, of which just 750,000 would be forthcoming. The calling-up of the 1919 class and other measures was not sufficient. By the end of the year, it had been necessary to disband twenty-five divisions; the army had fallen from over 2 million to around 1,670,000. It was even necessary to have front-line trenches held by men of the age of 40 or over, with some as old as 48. The shortage of men was ameliorated by an increase in artillery and a more careful use of manpower by many commanders.

The German Spring Offensive fell upon British-held positions. The attack was strong enough to push the British back with heavy casualties and loss of equipment. Initially the French army ignored Haig's requests for help but soon it was realised how dangerous the situation was and Pétain sent three divisions, later increased by a further six and then four more, still seven short of the requested number. As a result of this crisis, Foch was appointed overall commander of the Allied armies in France, but with tactical command still retained by each country's commander-in-chief, Haig, Pershing and Pétain.

On 25 March, the French halted the German advance near Noyon and rushed extra troops up to hold the Picardy sector with orders not to lose another metre. Troops were brought from Champagne and as far away as Italy. Although some territory was lost, the British and French divisions covered each other as they withdrew south of the Somme. As the German offensive wound down, the French were restoring the link to the British flank, and indeed the French 6th Army was attacking on the Oise.

The German Operation Georgette, launched on 9 April, did not fare as well as Operation Michael launched a month earlier. It was contained by the British in the south and by a joint British and French force, but not without the loss of Mount Kemmel by the French. The situation was stabilised by the arrival of eight infantry divisions, two cavalry corps and divisions from the reserve. The next German offensive would be against the French.

After returning to being a quiet front in October 1917, the Aisne once again found itself an important position during the Spring Offensive of 1918. It was held by just four French divisions which in May had been reinforced by three battered British divisions, sent there to rest. The German offensive, designed to capture the area and bring the French divisions supporting the British away from the area, was to be launched by 43 divisions containing many élite formations and over 4,000 guns. A small number of captured tanks were also to be used.

The French intended that the position should be held because of the losses in taking the Chemin des Dames but, 'stunned by the hurricane bombardment, the Allied units were dislocated by the German infiltration tactics and paralysed by the superior tempo of the attack. As the defence fell apart, the onslaught flooded over the plateau and beyond the Aisne.' Unfortunately the French troops had been massed in the front line where German artillery caused considerable casualties.

Using huge ladders the Germans crossed the Marne. In the confusion, the French did not blow the Aisne bridges, thereby allowing German troops to cross. A Breton division frustrated the German advance in the west but, in the east, where the order had been given to evacuate Reims, the situation was only saved by the timely arrival of troops from Picardy and other divisions scraped together by Pétain. Noting the assistance to the French of two American divisions, the Germans called the attack off, but followed this up with an attack between Montdidier and Noyon. The initial attack was very successful but was held by a vigorous counter-attack on the River Matz by Général Mangin's troops. Not long before the armistice the Chemin des Dames once more fell into Allied hands.

The next German offensive was again in Champagne. The three-army attack opened on 16 July with fifty-two divisions depleted by casualties and influenza. Facing them were four French armies and some American and Italian troops. Two French armies broke and, although they were held in the east, in the south-west the Germans again crossed the Marne, creating a bridgehead 12 kilometres long and 7 kilometres deep.

With almost total surprise, the French counter-attack between the Aisne and the Ourcq, which included American and British divisions, forced an orderly German withdrawal. With the French troops neither trained nor prepared to follow up, the Germans skilfully retired and prepared a defensive line between Vesle and the Aisne.

'Foch believed the best strategy for the Allies would now comprise a series of co-ordinated and sustained attacks with limited aims, none decisive but each preparing the way for the next, along the entire front, together with offensives in Italy and Macedonia.' The first, a joint British-French attack near Amiens, began on 8 August. With numerical superiority against weak divisions, it was a success, but the Allies were unable to keep up the momentum.

Général Mangin's attack on 17 August developed into a successful assault between the Aisne and the Oise. A further attack by Mangin's troops, coordinated with British assaults, forced a German withdraw from their intended winter positions. American success in the Saint-Mihiel salient was mirrored by Mangin in the Aisne sector where the Germans were pushed back to the Ailette River. Further attacks by the British and French brought the Allies within striking distance of the Hindenburg Line.

On 26 September, the French and Americans launched an offensive along the Meuse in the Argonne Forest which was met by spirited German defence. By the 29th the attack had been stopped with just a few kilometres gained. Almost simul-taneously the British had attacked at Cambrai and St. Quentin and the Belgians on the coast. Then on the 30th a new French assault began on the Aisne.

French troops assisted in the British attack at Cambrai, forcing the Germans back from the Hindenburg line. By 10 October, the French and Americans had cleared the Argonne Forest and began to advance up the Meuse. In quick succession Laon and the Chemin des Dames fell to French troops.

By November, the British and French armies were exhausted, allowing the Germans to retreat in relatively good order behind 'effective rear-guard actions'. The next French offensive was forestalled by the armistice. Foch had planned a massive offensive to take Lorraine, beginning on 14 November.

(**Opposite, above**) In France, every man was required to do military service after which they transferred to the Territorials (Reserve). Each year reservists were called up for a summer camp. This group are reservists during the summer camp, 1914. They are wearing the standard blue greatcoat and red trousers with early-style field boots. When this photograph was taken the war was only weeks away.

(**Opposite, below**) Another group of reservists, this time during their 1913 camp. While it was inconvenient for their families and employers, these men do not look too unhappy about their circumstances. At rest, the men are wearing white fatigues.

Camp de Bois Levêque M^{lle} et M^{al} 30 Juin - 1-2-3 Juillet 1913 L Cadi

(**Left**) A soldier of the 8th Regiment of Dragoons in full uniform taken in 1913. At the start of the war he would have worn the same uniform, with a dulled breast plate and a cloth cover on the helmet.

(**Right**) A soldier of the 171st Infantry Regiment posing before going off to war. He is wearing a dark blue double-breasted greatcoat over his single-breasted blue tunic. His regiment is shown on the collar and on the front of his cap. His rifle is the model 1886/93 Lebel.

Soldiers recalled on the outbreak of war often, patriotically, made their way to their regimental depots before the papers had arrived.

Troops assembled for boot inspection by the colonel of the regiment in Place Saint-François-Xavier, Paris, in August 1914.

(**Opposite, top**) After the boot inspection, the men wait for further orders. Like their German counterparts, many took their regimental flag with them to the front. The loss of the flag in battle was a severe black mark on the regiment and a real prize for the enemy.

(**Opposite, middle**) On receipt of orders to leave for the front, the regiment marched to Gare de l'Est. They were given a sound farewell by the assembled crowds. It is interesting to compare this with photographs of German troops leaving for the front.

(**Opposite, bottom**) France had a large empire, like Britain, and was able to mobilise troops from across the globe. The first to arrive were troops from North Africa. Here Algerian *Tirailleurs*, part of XIX Corps, are seen embarking on 10 August for France.

(**Above**) Algerian troops with their French officers, marching through Paris on their way to the front. Although visually appealing, their uniforms were totally unsuited to the rigours of the Western Front.

After being checked for complete equipment, prior to leaving for the front, a platoon of Infantry Regiment 147 pose for a farewell photograph. They have not yet been issued with a cap cover so the regimental number is seen on their collars and on the front of the cap. With the high casualty rate suffered in the opening months of the war, by the end of the year many in the photo would be dead.

Men to be reckoned with: a group of the Foreign Legion on their arrival in France. Normally they would not leave Africa but their fighting ability was needed on the Western Front. They are wearing standard French infantry clothing.

*140ᵐᵉ Territorial 7ᵐᵉ Compagnie. 6ᵐᵉ Escouade.*

The 140th Territorial Regiment was from the south of France where the weather was much milder than the north. They are pictured enjoying the weather in August 1914 shortly after arriving near the front.

Another group of territorials, this time complete with Regimental Banner and medals. The picture clearly shows how unwieldy for use in the trenches the rifle and bayonet must have been.

Elderly members of Infantry Regiment 53 on their way to the front. Note the different tunic worn by the man standing second from right.

Men too old to fight formed the Garde Civile, an armed organisation that guarded bridges and other important points behind the front. They wore civilian clothes with a white tunic over and an armband showing they were not franc-tireurs. Some wore the standard pattern military uniform.

A mixed group of the Garde Civile (GC) in full military uniform of various types. Some are wearing GC armbands, those without display regimental numbers on caps or collars; a few are wearing both. For an unknown reason they are not all wearing the same numerals.

The response to the mobilisation order was rapid and, very quickly, units were leaving for the front. This is the Territorial Infantry Regiment 30 marching to the station.

Some units left their depots with more fanfare than others. This is the march past of a Chasseurs Alpins battalion. They are wearing the distinctive chasseurs hat.

A column of infantry marching through the centre of Le Mans in August 1914; they are probably the 117th Infantry Regiment, the local garrison.

Infantry following the retreating Germans through Amiens at the end of September 1914; the town was in German hands for a month.

Infantry marching to the front. Few of the townspeople are out to wish them well; it was business as usual in the town.

Even with a war on and the Germans not far away, the grapes in the Champagne region still needed gathering. The harvest would rely on the young and old as most of the able-bodied men had been called up.

Algerian Spahis (cavalry) parading in Veurne in Belgium before moving to the front.

French Dragoons leaving Gembloux on reconnaissance. Note the parade ground helmets and tunics.

Infantry and mounted patrols meet in a wood.

Regular troops about to set up a bivouac for the night in August 1914.

Regular infantry at a halt on their way to the front.

It was more comforting for troops on their way to the front to rest in a town.

A group of Dragoons on their way to the front in a private car; their shiny helmets are covered in cloth to prevent them glinting in the sun.

Algerian *Tirailleurs*, called defensive regiments by the Germans, on their way to the front in the north of France. They are wearing a picturesque uniform only suited to warm climates.

A posed photo of Zouaves firing from behind a hedge. In the warmth of August and September 1914 their uniforms were not a problem but with cold weather they offered no protection to the wearer.

The original caption read 'a countryman offers a drink to a courier'.

A group of Zouaves that became detached in Laigue forest during the Battle of Vic-sur-l'Aisne.

Zouaves at a halt on their way to the front. The original is hand-coloured to show the bright uniforms worn by African troops: bright blue hat, red pantaloons, blue shirt with white sleeves and short blue jacket faced in red. In the attack they were highly visible and easy targets.

On 7 August, a French cavalry corps entered Belgium. Some of the troops are seen being welcomed by the residents in a village near the border.

French mountain troops in the Vosges mountains where the only sure way to move materials was by mule or manpower.

Infantry at rest and at the front are two St. Étienne M1907 machine guns.

As early as 11 September, Joffre recommended Maunoury move his forces from the right bank of the Oise to outflank the German right wing. It was necessary to build a temporary bridge to aid movement.

This rather ramshackle bridge was constructed in just nine hours between 10.00pm and 7.00am by a company of telephone engineers and thirty civilians.

On 17 September, 18,000 men of XIII Corps crossed, their objective being Noyon.

Unfortunately, German shelling, and a shortage of French munitions with which to respond, prevented a successful operation.

In the early stages of the war, the French method of attack was to rush at the German positions hoping that élan and fighting spirit would win the day. The high casualty rate indicated that it did not always work.

Although not as successful as hoped, the initial months saw the French liberate parts of Alsace-Lorraine. Here mountain troops are seen removing the border marker between German Elsaß-Lothringen and France.

Fort Troyon was part of the Verdun defences. The defenders held out for three days and helped stop the German advance across the Meuse and around Verdun. Its defence created the St. Mihiel salient.

In order to get troops across the Marne, a bridge had to be made. Here boats can be seen, used to create a floating road suitable for men to cross on. Interestingly the boats are being brought in by civilians, some of whom have bicycles; no doubt to get home on.

Although the Noyon offensive had not been successful, it yielded many prisoners; some of which are seen here being marched in the direction of Compiègne. The prisoners are being escorted by dismounted cavalry.

Considerable numbers of men were taken prisoner on both sides during the opening moves of the war. These are French soldiers being marched to a rail junction for transportation to Germany.

CÔTÉ DU MIDI

50. La Guerre Européenne 1914 — Le 7 Octobre 1914 on app... aux Inv...les
six drapeaux pris aux Allemands a la Bataille de l'Aisn... "Phot-Express

A number of French and German regiments took their regimental flags into the front line. They were highly prized as trophies and were displayed along with captured hardware. Here, six flags captured during the Battle of the Aisne are displayed.

The Garde Civile, in uniform and civilian clothing, are here waiting, in prepared positions, to defend their village.

(**Opposite, above**) French mountain troops in the Vosges Mountains wait for the expected German attack.

(**Opposite, below**) Troops eat a hasty meal in the trenches while one soldier looks out for an attack.

(**Above**) As trench warfare took hold, the trenches took a more permanent appearance. To make sure the sides did not collapse, especially during wet weather, they were propped up with whatever was at hand; these are held up with chicken wire and include covered loopholes for snipers.

Here French artillerists, working behind the line, are checking and cleaning each individual shell before it leaves the depot. During busy periods, the movement of shells would have been too rapid for such a process.

The shells, seen being loaded into a limber in the previous photo, would then have been taken to the field guns, which are here seen being put in position to fire.

In the early days of mobile warfare, guns were set up quickly and moved with the flow of the battle. Here a battery of 75s is being set up.

This LL postcard shows a 75 battery in action on the Ypres front.

(**Above**) A French 75 battery in action, showing clearly the distance between each gun.

(**Opposite, top**) Here a sole 75 gun is firing at a farm occupied by the Germans.

(**Opposite, middle**) Heavy artillery also took up any position where it was needed during the opening months of the war. Here a battery is taking up position prior to firing.

(**Opposite, bottom**) Less portable were the heavy mortars which were taken off their wheels for firing. This is a 220mm heavy mortar on its base plate, used to absorb the recoil force, about to be fired.

A heavy French artillery battery in action; each gun has been given a name: at the front is Kolossal and behind Kultur.

Each gun had to be manhandled into position. The 155mm gun was not especially large compared to some guns which needed dismantling for transport and could take a day to put together.

Communication between the front and headquarters was done by telephone whenever it was possible. These are telephone engineers testing newly-laid equipment in a village behind the front.

French colonial soldiers with foot problems wait for their fellow soldiers to unload the baggage wagon before they can be evacuated. This picture was taken somewhere in the Vosges region.

(**Above**) A group of clerics behind the front. Although not in uniform, they all are wearing a Red Cross armband so are probably attached to a medical unit. Three religions are represented: on the left are two Catholic priests, in the centre is a Protestant pastor, and on the right is a rabbi.

(**Opposite, above**) It was not uncommon for both sides to pose with their captives. In the centre is a captive German infantryman. The photograph was taken towards the end of 1914.

(**Opposite, below**) This photo was taken in Souain on 21 December 1914 at 0830 hrs. The men are having breakfast just an hour before going into battle.

(**Opposite, above**) Three important men and their attendants. In the centre is Joffre, to his left is Pau, and to his right is Castelnau. On the left of the picture is Beschauer.

(**Above, left**) Not all French generals stayed behind the lines. Général Villaret was seriously wounded by a sniper near Reims on 13 March 1915.

(**Opposite, below**) French troops on their way to the front, watched by three generals. At the front is Joffre, and behind him Foch and Dubail.

(**Above, right**) Another general who was wounded was Général Maunoury. He was shot through the eye and partially blinded while touring the front on 11 March 1915. The wound was severe enough to end his career.

Joffre, meeting with regimental and divisional staff sometime in 1915.

An unusual photo in any army: this is Général de Division Marchand in a supposedly front-line trench.

Field hospitals were not always a building or set of tents. These men are stretcher bearers, part of 4 Ambulance which was situated at Loemart Farm on 2 December 1914.

Unloading wounded men at Boulogne dock. It is a confusing photo with some wounded coming from the ship, stretchers on the ground, a wounded man being loaded into a wagon, and Red Cross wagons at the back; they are unconverted goods wagons like that in the following photograph.

The original caption to this is simple: 'on the way to hospital'. Although certainly in a lot of pain, they are clearly happy with their lot.

The staff of a military hospital situated in the grounds of a château.

Lightly wounded men being looked after in a wealthy civilian's house.

(**Above**) Three infantrymen pose in front of a wrecked building in the late spring of 1915.

(**Opposite, above**) North African troops at rest behind the lines. The man, standing second from left, is sporting a business-like knife.

(**Opposite, below**) A group of seven men of the 21st Regiment; their rank badges suggest they are artillery. Note the different tunic worn by the cyclist, and his cape. In the centre is a sergeant and on the far right a corporal.

During the period when the 1914 uniform was being replaced by the 1915 uniform, many soldiers wore corduroy.

Men of the 405th Infantry Regiment machine gun section wearing the new 1915 uniform and a distinguishing badge on the upper arm to show their role.

Somewhere in Picardy, Spahis and their mounts bring back a stray horse.

Lord Kitchener, seen here inspecting North African troops, is exchanging words with a Spahi officer. According to the original caption the photo was taken seventeen years after the Fashoda incident of September 1898.

The German caption for this photo read: 'a French soldier on a small vehicle acting as an outpost on the Somme'. The two floats have holes for standing in and a small wooden chair is provided for what must have been a very precarious job. How he could signal if he saw anything was not explained.

Two forward observation soldier-release pigeons with important information attached to their legs. Many thousands were used, a large number of which were killed by crack shots and shellfire.

According to the German caption, this is a French outpost in the Argonne. It looks rather too substantial to be an outpost, and is more likely an encampment for troops out of the line.

(**Opposite, above**) A battlefield burrow on the wooded Meuse. This is a shell-proof dugout behind the first line of trenches in the Verdun sector. It was used as an ammunition store. The roof is screened with cut branches to disguise it from aerial view. For some unknown reason, the Chasseur Alpin is unscrewing the nose cap off a shell.

(**Opposite, below**) Alpine troops resting in a secure shelter in the Vosges Mountains.

(**Above**) The main street through a village created by soldiers: Bon Espoir. It consisted of a dozen hutments arranged around a village square. Each villa had a name such as 'Mon Plaisir' and 'Terreur des Boches'.

(**Above**) Bon Espoir also had a camp barber who worked in the open-air when the weather was fine, but in one of the straw huts when it rained.

(**Opposite, above**) A group of pioneers taking a rest during the construction of new trenches in the Vosges Mountains.

(**Opposite, below**) Troops taking Mass behind the lines.

Loading and firing a large mortar required a team of men.

As aerial reconnaissance increased, it became necessary to camouflage gun positions whenever possible. This is a camouflaged heavy gun in position in the Champagne.

Part of the crew for this heavy field gun pose along with two of the types of shell fired.

Men from the 40th Regiment wearing the 1915 uniform pose with a machine gunner from the 11th Regiment, who is still wearing the pre-war uniform. The machine gun is the St. Étienne M 1907.

A simple method of throwing grenades a longer distance was to use a catapult. It could be done from cover, giving the operator a level of safety.

To the British, a trench mortar, to the Germans, Minenwerfer, to the French these were aerial torpedoes known as *crapouillots*. They came in various sizes and could deliver a considerable payload. The men who fired them were considered to be an élite unit.

(**Above**) Infantry on the march to rear positions. All armies used mules to carry loads because of their strength.

(**Opposite, above**) Pictured during the Battle of Champagne, shelters and cantonment of a Zouave regiment.

(**Opposite, below**) Construction of trenches in the rear positions, quite some way back from the front, as the men are walking around quite freely.

(**Below**) Replenishing an artillery unit with shells.

GUERRE DE 1914–1915
Ravitaillement d'obus sur la ligne de feu

The further back from the front, the more elaborate the trench system could be. This one boasts a shower room.

Early trenches were often straight, not very deep and lacked the defensive measures adopted later.

As trenches became deeper to provide greater protection, it was necessary to have a fire step to stand on at stand-to when an attack might be expected or when a German assault occurred. The constant threat from snipers when men used the fire step meant that periscopes were needed to see into no man's land.

(**Above, left**) A photograph taken on 24 May 1915 shows that there was communication by placards and signs between the opposing sides. Literally translated, the two signs read: 'Italy is with us' and 'God is dead in Reims' but the original French caption translated the latter into 'Your God died in Reims'.

(**Above, right**) A front-line trench taken from a communication trench. A Chasseur Alpin is watching no man's land from behind an earth parapet; another soldier, not on duty, is posing in his funk hole, cut into the side of the trench; and a third soldier stands at the ready and is watching through a slit in the sand bags.

(**Right**) This trench photo was taken allegedly somewhere near Nieuport. It is of a better construction with a wooden fire step, wooden buttresses to hold back the earth, and intermeshed twigs to provide cover while allowing the troops to fire through them.

The first gas masks were simple affairs as this picture shows: a cotton pad impregnated with anti-gas chemicals and a set of glasses. The soldier standing is about to throw a grenade so the German trenches must be quite close.

This photograph shows the effects of gas before rudimentary precautions were taken. The caption read: 'Zouaves surprised behind their parapet by a gas cloud are sleeping the sleep without end'.

Troops posing in a shell-damaged building to show the new improved gas mask. Unlike that in the previous photo, it is all in one piece and has an aluminium respirator on the front, but it is still only held on by a single strap.

In a recently recaptured trench at Souchez near Arras, men are searching their clothes for lice. The French caption read: 'the Germans have left but their lice stayed' and the English translation was given as: 'searching for German lice'. Almost certainly they would have brought their own lice with them as many soldiers were lousy.

Général Joffre, inspecting soldiers wearing the newly introduced Adrian helmet.

A photo taken in the trenches prior to the start of the Champagne offensive in September 1915. The original French caption read: '09.12, 25 September 1915'. On the fire step of the forward trench, men of the colonial infantry wait for the signal to go over the top.

Taken from the trenches just left by the attackers, the photo shows the colonial troops advancing on the German positions. They appear to be advancing as if they are on manoeuvres and within less than an hour had moved forward 2.5 kilometres.

In some places no man's land was kilometres wide. This photo purports to be of an attack by a French patrol in Lorraine.

Although attacking under machine gun fire, the first wave is here seen in the newly captured German positions.

These are trenches at Bois Brûlé on 6 April during a German counter-attack. The men can be seen rushing to meet the threat during which the adjutant, Péricard, muttered the cry: 'Stand the dead'.

Dug in along the road from Lizerne to Boesinghe on 24 April 1915, these Zouaves are only 150 metres from the German outposts.

This wounded French soldier was lucky. He was found between the lines by a group of sappers, two days after the attack.

A wounded soldier is being attended by a female nurse and orderly at a field dressing station behind the trenches.

For most of the time, cavalry were used as dismounted troops, but they came in handy when there were numbers of prisoners to escort. These Algerian Spahis are escorting German PoWs during the 1915 campaign in Flanders.

During periods of rest from the trenches, like all soldiers, they were set to work clearing up after the battle had moved on. This is the village of Maixe on 24 December 1914.

Senegalese troops taking a break on the way to the front.

The French contributed troops to the Gallipoli campaign and in the Balkans. These native troops are in the trenches on the Gallipoli peninsula. In the centre is the divisional commander who is talking with the white officers of the battalion.

Some French units took their flags to war. This photo, taken in a Turkish cemetery at Sedd el Bahr, shows the flag of a colonial regiment with its guard.

Two generals posing like their men would on a captured Turkish gun at Sedd el Bahr fort. On the right is Général Gouraud who lost his right arm during the Gallipoli campaign and sitting is Général Bailloud, commander of 156th Infantry Division, who replaced Gouraud when he was wounded. As here Gouraud has both arms, the photo was taken before 30 June 1915.

(**Above, left**) Another photo of Général Gouraud, this time with two staff officers, one French and one British (right).

(**Opposite, above**) French colonial troops during a rest in the fighting on 21 June 1915. The officers of the battalion are discussing their next attack.

(**Above, right**) By 1916 every soldier should have been in the M1915 uniform. This photo, sent by a French soldier in Infantry Regiment 129, to his English wife in September 1916 shows that it was not always so. He is wearing corduroy rather than horizon blue trousers; not uncommon, even a year after their introduction.

(**Opposite, below**) Colonial infantry in front of what appears to be a German railway wagon. They are dressed in a khaki, tropical style, uniform. The photograph gives no clue to where they are.

Annamite troops from the French colonies in Southeast Asia. As colonial troops they had their own uniform, in this case, in khaki. Most were used in labour battalions but some held support trenches.

Soldiers from Tonkin, northern Vietnam, are shown resting at a Paris station on their way to the front. They are wearing a very traditional style of headwear.

The flag carriers of a North African regiment displaying their company colours. As a Muslim regiment, the tri-coloured edged fanions had crescent-topped flagpoles and a 'spread hand' symbol with fingers extended (a mystic sign designed to ward off evil spirits).

For the French forces the greatest battle of 1916, both strategically and politically, was for Verdun. Here a lorry column is passing through a village behind Verdun, moving material to the front.

(**Opposite, above**) Most soldiers from Indo-China were used behind the lines. Here they are driving a convoy of necessities for the men at the front under the direction of a French officer.

(**Opposite, below**) Many forms of transport had been used by the French army to get troops to the front in 1914 to defend Paris. Here, nearly two years later, Paris buses are still in use to bring troops to the front.

(**Above**) The French army maintained probably the most complete messenger-pigeon service of all the major combatants. Here, somewhere on the Vosges Front, pigeons are being loaded into baskets for transport to the front where they were used to send messages back.

(**Above**) To keep in touch with aeroplane observers and take in messages from intermediate stations and bases, the French army set up frontline wireless stations close behind the battlefront.

(**Opposite**) A cavalryman in 1916: a modern warrior in a medieval helmet and lance.

(**Right**) Even during the battle for Verdun, soldiers were given some respite from the front. This is an underground theatre equipped with electric light and decked with tricolours.

*Equipe de football du 5 Cuirassiers*
*SP 224*

*Capitaine de l'equipe*

Behind the lines, during rest periods, there was time for organised sport. The preferred sport for most was football. This is a typical soldiers' squad from the 5th Cuirassiers; the team captain is at the bottom left.

With lice and mud commonplace, out of the line, most soldiers tried to get as clean as possible. Here some soldiers wash their clothes while others use the water to cool their feet, or sail boats.

Behind the lines, non-infantry personnel had more free time. To stave off boredom they pursued a range of interests. This poilu is making violins out of shell cases and wood.

Wounded men being rewarded for their bravery at a medal presentation in a base hospital.

(**Opposite, above**) A column of infantry marching towards the sound of the guns.

(**Opposite, below left**) A communication trench was used to get men to the front without being seen. They had to start some distance away from the front to keep the men hidden. These men are at the entrance to such a trench which is steadily getting deeper.

(**Opposite, below right**) A private in the 121st Infantry Regiment standing outside his deep dugout in the Vosges sector during the winter of 1916. He is wearing a M1915 tunic and forage cap, and leather gaiters.

(**Above**) In the mountainous forested regions, it was possible to build walkways which would survive the weather.

This is shelter number 10, built into the side of a hill to provide maximum protection against the weather and shells.

A shallow early trench which has been sturdily built to stop the sides collapsing, but is too shallow for protection against snipers.

When time and the local terrain allowed, dugouts could be very substantial. These are medical dugouts in the Champagne region.

These are French hillside dugouts near Verdun.

Like their British and German counterparts, officers' dugouts were usually better equipped and more comfortable than those for other ranks.

While their officers dined in style, the poilu ate out of a mess tin in the trench.

Hot food was prepared away from the trenches and carried to them in large containers. Where possible it was prepared in the rear trenches so individual troops could collect their ration. Here hot food is being served in a rear trench.

To contain any enemy infiltration, trench junctions were often fitted with a drop-down barbed wire gate and overhead barbed wire.

(**Above**) A timber and wire netting barricade placed across trenches to stop enemy infiltration during trench raids.

(**Above right**) From 1915 gas was an ever present threat, even during quiet times. Each side developed their own ways of warning troops. This unit used a klaxon horn.

(**Right**) This image shows clearly how the terrain was used defensively. An officer's dugout carved deeply into a hillside.

(**Opposite, above**) A supply depot, behind the front, well-stocked for the Arras offensive.

(**Opposite, below**) The French army used thousands of shells a day. Such a rate of expenditure required many dumps like this one.

(**Above**) A pneumatic grenade thrower that propelled the bomb a considerable distance and that could be safely sited without giving away the firer's position.

A French anti-aircraft gun somewhere on the Western Front.

Trench mortars were fired from positions in the trench system where they could not be observed. This meant manhandling the bombs through the trench system to their destination. This could be a difficult and lengthy process, especially for a heavy mortar, because the bombs for a heavy mortar could only be carried one at a time.

As snipers disguised their positions carefully, it is unusual to see a photograph of one in action. This is posed to show how they worked. Later in the war they would wear camouflage suits to avoid detection.

Phote Georges — Reprod Interd.

A St. Étienne 8mm machine gun section in action during 1916 in Morocco. As well as fighting against the Germans, the French also had to maintain forces in their colonies to keep order. Some of the men are wearing tropical pith helmets which ventilated at the top.

Large field guns fired very heavy shells many kilometres and needed a considerable number of men and specialised equipment to function. Here a soldier is helping load a 370mm gun.

Another view of the mechanism needed to move a large calibre shell.

A British medical officer is seen holding a magazine for the St. Étienne machine gun, positioned for anti-aircraft defence. Behind him is another British officer who is holding the machine gun.

Vue prise n° 335

35. GUERRE 1914-1916. — Bataille de la Somme.
Dépôt de munitions d'artillerie. - Chargement de caissons.
Dépôt of artillery ammunitions - Loading ammunitions. - L

(**Opposite, above**) French ordnance in action: a 4.8 inch field gun was technically heavy artillery but was nothing in comparison with many other guns.

(**Opposite, below**) Taken during the Battle of the Somme, this shows a munitions depot where empty caissons were filled and sent back to the battery.

(**Above**) Two 75mm guns in their emplacements immediately to the rear of Fort Douaumont. Working on a revolving emplacement meant it was easy to reposition the gun as needed. Each battery was connected with Headquarters by phone, allowing the whole mass of artillery to be concentrated on one point at the general's command.

A demonstration of the Brandt grenade thrower. This piece of trench artillery was designed by Frenchman Edgar Brandt in 1916. It used compressed air to fire the projectile.

In the Vosges, a tree stump was a ready-made mount for an anti-aircraft gun (in this case a St. Étienne infantry machine gun).

A large trench mortar about to be fired by just one man. The rest of the team are safe around a traverse in the trench.

This is captioned in the original German illustration as a French 80mm mountain cannon used for throwing mines. Mortar shells shaped like this moved quite slowly because they were not very aerodynamic. When it was spotted, its likely impact point could be predicted, giving men time to take shelter.

During the 1917 German retreat, heavy guns had to be moved to follow up the advance. This gun is being pulled by a gun tractor, in this case a lorry.

Some guns were mounted on narrow gauge railway wagons to facilitate their movement. This 120mm piece is hidden in a wood to avoid German spotter planes.

The war underground was just as dangerous as the war above ground. This photograph clearly shows the cramped conditions the engineer miners worked in. There are no props for the ceiling so a cave-in is obviously not expected: it is solid rock.

THE SOLDIERS' DAILY LIFE
A BATTLEFIELD GAME OF CARDS

Behind the lines, while waiting to go forward, there were no tasks to complete to keep the soldiers amused. While most just sit and wait, one group is playing cards.

It was essential to stay hydrated so barrels of water were placed in communication trenches.

(**Above**) These strange objects are portable circular segments of a trench turret. The turrets were made of steel armour and were for setting up at sharp bends in the lines, or points of vantage, with machine guns inside.

(**Right**) The trench turret could also be used as an air raid shelter for sentries.

(**Opposite, above**) Men well back from the front wait for the order to move forward.

(**Opposite, below**) This group of men are waiting for the order that will propel them into the fighting around Verdun.

128

The columns marching to and from Verdun seemed to be endless. Here a new artillery regiment is making its way to the front.

Well back from the front, shown by the number of fires, a group of infantry wait their turn to fight at Verdun.

FRENCH INFANTRY IN RESERVE AT VERDUN.

A new infantry regiment moves to the front. They are marching through a village to the strains of the national anthem. The photo was taken a few days after the Verdun battle began.

A French cavalry regiment on the march during the Somme battles. No indication of what they were about to do was given.

Millions of shells were fired during the Verdun battle, creating a lunar landscape that would be repeated during the Third Battle of Ypres the following year.

This is Lieutenant Colonel Driant who was killed during the battle for Bois des Caures on 22 February 1916. After nearly two days of very heavy fighting, his two battalions of chasseurs were surrounded and had the choice of surrendering or attempting to make their way back to the French lines. He ordered them to break out and, during this, he was hit while attending a wounded soldier. It was reported his last words were: 'Oh! Là, Mon Dieu!' His stand had held up the Germans for 24 hours and bought the French defences extra time.

The ground around Fort Souville after the German assault had been checked.

A French sentry posted at the entrance to Fort Souville, wearing a gas mask because there was no one to warn him.

What Fort Vaux looked like after the German bombardment, with each possible entry point protected by sandbags and guards.

To move along his army's front, Pétain used a train in which he had a carriage converted to an office (it also made it easier for his staff to be with him). He is pictured seated at his desk in the train's office.

Général Joffre and Pétain on a visit to Verdun during the battle.

(**Above, left**) Général Nivelle played an important part in holding the German assault on Verdun. As a result of this success he was promoted over many senior officers to succeed Joffre. His plans to win the war in April/May 1917 failed and he was replaced by Pétain. In December 1917 he was transferred to North Africa.

(**Above, right**) The city of Verdun also came under bombardment during the battle. Important points inside the city were guarded by sentries and protected with sandbags to reduce damage from blasts.

(**Right**) A photograph of Rue Mazel, which, when compared with the next photo, is barely damaged. It also clearly illustrates the long periods of waiting around experienced by soldiers, who are here sitting among the ruins.

French soldiers are here taking a break from their job of clearing the streets of bomb and shell damage. On the right is a despatch rider.

French cavalry practising for the big advance and patrolling in Picardy.

Two French soldiers in a re-taken trench at Maucourt during the Somme offensive. Behind them are the ruins of the château.

Almost certainly a posed picture: rushing 75mm guns up during the Somme advance.

The state of some of the trenches taken over from the French in the Somme region.

French military telephone engineers laying an underground phone line in Cappy on the Somme.

French engineers placing telephone wires across the newly re-taken village of Dompierre.

Cavalry at rest. The photograph was taken between Curlu and Hem in the Somme region in 1916. The panorama shows the battle-damaged landscape and the German trench lines.

Vue Paris n° 331
GUERRE 1914-1916. — Bataille de la Somme
Curlu-Hem. — Vue d'ensemble d'une ancienne ligne de défense
allemandes. — A view of german defences — LL.

Vue Paris n° 833
833 GUERRE 1914-1916. — Bataille de la Somme. — Tilloloy. — L'Hospice après le bombardement. — The almshouse after the bombardment — LL.

The alms house in Tilloloy during the Somme offensive.

A colonel is seen here issuing orders from his desk on 29 September 1915 during the Battle of Champagne.

During a battle, the trenches were often clogged with the dead, dying, wounded and equipment. To add to the difficulties of moving the wounded, many trenches were narrow and shell-damaged.

French troops in the jump-off trench during the 1917 Champagne battle are watching the barrage they will soon have to follow.

War is a messy business and leaves behind things that need removing. Shortly after the French wave had moved on during the 1917 Champagne battle, follow-up troops had the job of making the trenches serviceable as the new reserve line. This required the removal of any German equipment, rebuilding damaged sections of trench and removing the dead.

On 18 August 1917, a
Moroccan colonial regiment
re-took the ruins of Fleury.
Here they are waiting in the
trenches after the assault,
waiting for a possible
counter-attack.

Just some of the 12,000 PoWs taken during the Champagne offensive.

(**Above, left**) Three over-sized Germans guarded by possibly one of the smallest soldiers in the French army.

(**Above, right**) Two French officers about to go out on a night-time patrol. They are dressed in black clothing to make them blend into the night.

For many of the dead, there was no time for their removal to an established cemetery. They were simply buried close to where they fell and their grave marked so they could be re-interred later. This soldier was lucky that there was a priest available to provide a final service.

LA
GRANDE VICTOIRE

SOMME
TRENTIN
BUKOVINE
VERDUN
CHAMPAGNE
MARNE

Il monte...

.........

il monte.....

........LE BAROMÈTRE DE LA VICTOIRE

210

A postcard produced after the initial French victories on the Somme showing how close they felt to final victory: 'it's climbing … it's climbing … the barometer of Victory'.

A late-war machine gun company which, when compared with the photo on page 38, clearly shows the changes that had occurred in the French army. The latter look like seasoned troops dressed for modern warfare.

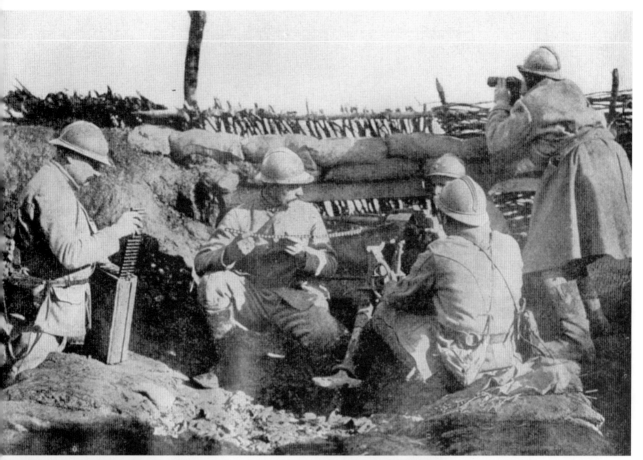

Firing the 8mm St. Étienne machine gun required a team of five men: a spotter, the gun operator, and three men to deal with the ammunition. This is a machine gun detachment in action.

This 8mm Hotchkiss machine gun has been sunk into the ground and sandbagged to look like a well. It was designed to shoot down low-flying planes that often followed the same journey out and back.

Both sides used counter-battery suppression routinely but specifically before and during an offensive. Mixed with the high-explosive were gas shells intended to catch the unwary. Wearing gas masks made firing the gun more difficult.

In front of Montdidier, a battery of 75mm field guns in position.

In the mountainous regions it was not always possible to bring larger guns into action. These three men are bringing a mountain gun and ammunition limbers to the front.

(**Opposite, above**) When the German Spring Offensive ran out of steam, the Allies were quick to mount their own attacks. As a result it was essential for the artillery to keep up with the infantry to provide support. This 75mm battery, pictured on the evening of 18 July 1918, was being set up on ground that had been occupied by the Germans in the morning.

(**Opposite, below**) A gun tractor bringing forward a heavy gun during the Allied advance on the Aisne Front in 1918.

(**Above**) A French heavy gun in action.

Very heavy artillery needed to be dismantled before it could be moved. Often each piece required its own transport, as here with the barrel for the 240mm gun on one trailer and a small convoy behind carrying the other parts.

This truck is pulling the mounting for the gun in the photograph above.

The mounting for this heavy howitzer required two wagons.

A heavy 270mm howitzer in transit on one wagon. To put the parts together would require further equipment.

(**Opposite, above**) Some heavy artillery was carried by rail and set up, some was permanently mounted on a rail carriage for rapid movement. This is a heavy artillery piece that was permanently mounted on a train.

(**Opposite, below**) On firm ground it was possible to lay a track so that rail-mounted heavy guns could be positioned for maximum effect and then removed before retaliatory fire.

(**Above, left**) The biggest guns were rail-mounted and required a large crew to operate.

(**Above, right**) A camouflaged very heavy gun being made ready to fire.

(**Above**) Not all heavy guns were easily moveable. This long-range gun, in an underground emplacement, was in position in the Marne district. The gun was protected by sandbag revetments on both sides and a solid bombproof roof, supported by horizontal iron girders, so that only a direct frontal hit could damage the gun.

(**Right**) A large gun used on the Somme. The main picture shows a 16 inch gun in position and in the circle a gun of smaller calibre. The construction of hundreds of miles of track enabled the French to use heavy naval ordnance and 'monster' army howitzers, moving them rapidly to any point. The presence of a small child is a puzzle.

(**Opposite page**) A very heavy artillery piece in action. To an enemy aircraft the amount of smoke would easily pinpoint the firing point, so such large guns fired from long distances.

(**Above**) Once the narrow gauge railway finished, the transport of shells was by manpower. In this picture, a working party is transporting 220mm shells on four-handled ammunition trays. Each shell weighed 350 pounds. Smaller ammunition was carried from the railhead to the gun. This working party are carrying 155mm shells, weighing 100 pounds apiece.

(**Opposite, above**) Large gun ammunition was kept a short distance away. Because of the weight of the shells they were moved on small trolleys on very narrow gauge rails, towed by two men.

(**Opposite, below**) Once the heavy shells were close to the gun, a winch was used to bring the shell to the breech.

(**Above**) Like smaller ordnance, the heavy shells were kept at a dump until needed.

(**Opposite, above left**) A group of 1918 soldiers, in this case machine gunners of the 210th Infantry Regiment. They are wearing the standard M1915 horizon blue tunic and helmet and a double-pronged leather belt.

(**Opposite, above right**) A veteran soldier wearing a sheepskin jerkin, a casque Adrian and a large beard. The necktie is to stop the tunic rubbing his neck.

(**Opposite, below**) Veteran soldiers from the colonies. In the centre is the commanding officer of 2 Section, 3rd Moroccan Regiment. Only two of the officers are not wearing traditional Zouave headwear (a cylindrical red wool cap known as a *chéchia*). Two soldiers are wearing a coarse wool overcoat while the rest of the men are wearing the M1915 pattern horizon blue coat.

These five men were responsible for capturing twenty-seven prisoners during a successful raid on German positions on 14 July 1918. The five men were Lieutenant Balestier, Sergeant Lejeune, Corporals Gourmelon and Hoquet, and Private Aumasson.

French artillery batteries on the way to the front through a village on the Somme. The convoy coming in the opposite direction are empty ammunition wagons returning after delivering their loads during the night. There is a reminder to drive on the right posted on the post.

The mule is loaded with a machine gun and its mounting; the soldier crouching is in charge of the mule and load.

Among the many colonial soldiers employed on the Western Front were Annamites from Indo-China. Here they are loading trucks with ammunition. Interestingly the trucks are Italian.

(**Above**) Many colonial soldiers were used on lines-of-communication work, like this West African driver pictured moving material to the Somme Front.

(**Opposite, above**) When the Germans withdrew in 1917 and late 1918, they destroyed any bridges that were usable. As the Allies advanced, often under fire, they replaced them with trestle bridges which were quick to build.

(**Opposite, below**) With the return of a war of movement, cyclist troops could once again be used. Here a company of *chasseurs cyclistes* are resting after a long journey, during which they were in action.

(**Below**) A common practice where a road ran within possible view of the enemy was to hide movement behind a screen. This screened-off highway was on the Aisne Front.

Captured enemy soldiers are standing at ease, as are their guards, before entraining for life in a PoW camp.

A station in Salonika where a regiment is entraining for the front somewhere in Serbia. Between the crossed rifles is the regimental flag, closely guarded by four men.

A division moving forward stretched a long way. These infantry are lucky in being transported to the front instead of having to walk.

In order to reduce casualties, trench relief usually took place in the dark. This regiment is marching to the front in daylight so they are a long way back from the front line.

(**Opposite, above**) French colonial soldiers on their way to billets after a spell of duty in the front line. The regimental standard is being carried at the head of the column with a guard on each side.

(**Opposite, below**)The original caption for this photo indicates that it is a regiment returning to the front. It is therefore unusual to see any smiling on their return (centre), unless it was for the camera.

(**Above**) As well as laying mines in the road and booby traps, the Germans also cut down trees to block the roads. It was simple for infantry to get over the trunks but it effectively stopped motorised transport. Here engineers are cutting up the trunks into moveable pieces so the road can be cleared.

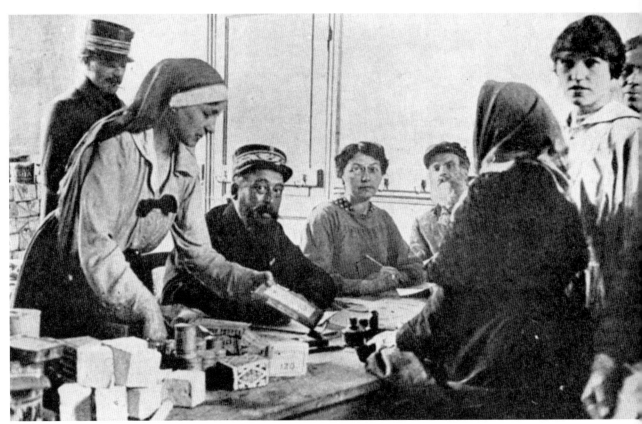

As the Allies advanced, they found people still living in many of the towns and villages. It was the army's responsibility to care for them in every way. Here, in Château Thierry, an army officer, assisted by a nurse, is distributing food.

During the 1917 withdrawal, the Germans turned destroyed buildings into fortified positions. This one was at Estrée-en-Chausée in the Somme region.

CAMPAGNE 1914-1917

Both sides made use of searchlights in the trenches to illuminate no man's land to help dazzle the defenders or illuminate a target for the artillery. They were vulnerable to enemy fire so had to be portable and were often placed in entrenchments for protection. This portable searchlight is being used by mountain troops in the Vosges Mountains.

Setting up a searchlight in the confined spaces of the trenches was clearly quite a task as this picture shows.

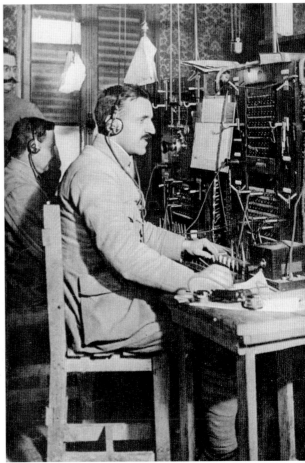

(**Above, left**) This telephone operator is working in a portable shelter designed to keep the weather out on three sides. For ease of movement and transport the structure was collapsible, and with the struts closed and the cross-battens disconnected, could be folded and easily carried. The lower transverse batten offered a seat for the operator, who could keep his message block or notebook hung beside him.

(**Above, right**) A French military telephone exchange somewhere in the Somme region. The shuttered windows and patterned wallpaper identify the exchange as a former private residence.

(**Opposite, above**) This illustrates some of the essential of trench life: war materiel in reserve at a depot in the Meuse sector. In the foreground can be seen the narrow-gauge rail tracks by which materiel is moved from the main railway lines.

(**Opposite, below**) An artesian well in a French camp sunk among the trees to evade aerial observation.

To assist artillery fire, both sides used observation balloons to direct fire. This is winching gear for a French balloon.

Observation balloons were moved deflated, and inflated close to where they would be anchored. Filling a large balloon required large amounts of gas. Similarly, releasing a poison gas cloud required a large number of cylinders. Without the rest of the picture it is hard to know what these cylinders were for. The German caption indicates they were poison gas.

Fortified positions provided safety when in range of long distance guns. These are some of the Verdun fortifications which provided shelter when out of the line.

Providing a safe environment required considerable amounts of time and material. These men are in the process of building an officer's post in a quarry somewhere on the Aisne Front.

This photograph was taken near Monastir on the Balkan Front and purports to show the roots of a tree being used as a dugout. The soldier is reading a letter from home.

These are the reserve trenches somewhere on the French front in northern France. What had been a large forest was now merely firewood.

Manual trench digging was slow, labour-intensive and back-breaking work. In positions where the enemy were unlikely to spot the creation of new trenches, it was possible to use machines.

A close-up of the trench digging equipment used by the French army in the later stages of the war.

Wooded areas were used by both sides to make things disappear from view. This is a field kitchen, belching smoke, unseen in a wood near Verdun.

This photo was taken after the French mutinies in 1917 and shows Pétain talking to men out of the lines for rest. He was responsible for an improvement in the soldiers' daily lives and for increasing leave.

To fend off boredom, some soldiers used their skills to fashion shells into lamps, flower vases, and just simple decorative pieces. This picture shows trench art in the making.

The Gare de l'Est was the station from which the greatest number of troops left for the front. Like the main London stations, it had rooms for the soldiers passing through. This is the dining facility for other ranks.

The sleeping arrangements for troops moving through the Gare de L'Est were equally as functional as the dining facilities.

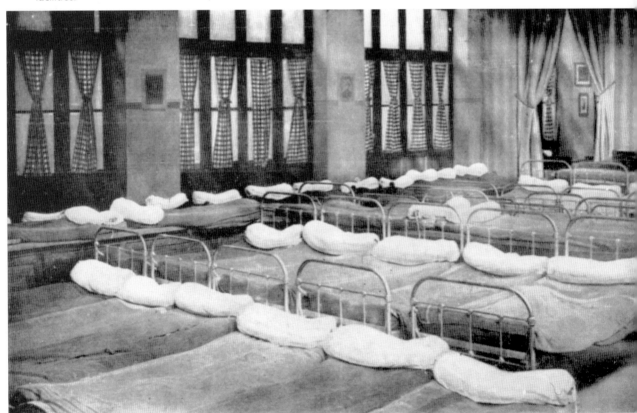

Général Joffre decorating twelve generals and a lone private with the Military Medal.

Général Nivelle and a British officer are awarding medals to the defenders of Verdun.

(**Opposite, above**) A group award ceremony for some of the defenders of Verdun.

(**Above**) The French Foreign Legion was noted for the bravery of its men. Here two be-medalled officers and three other ranks pose with their standard. For unit bravery, the Foreign Legion standard was decorated with the Legion of Honour, *Fourragère*, and six Croix de Guerre. The officer holding the flag is the regimental commandant.

(**Opposite, below**) Other units were also noted for their fighting prowess. These men are Moroccan *Tirailleurs* who just been presented with another medal for their collection.

Here, at a divisional parade, Général Gouraud is seen decorating a stretcher bearer.

As has been previously seen, whenever possible, food was prepared close to the front. Here it has been prepared behind the lines and is being carried forward to positions on the Somme.

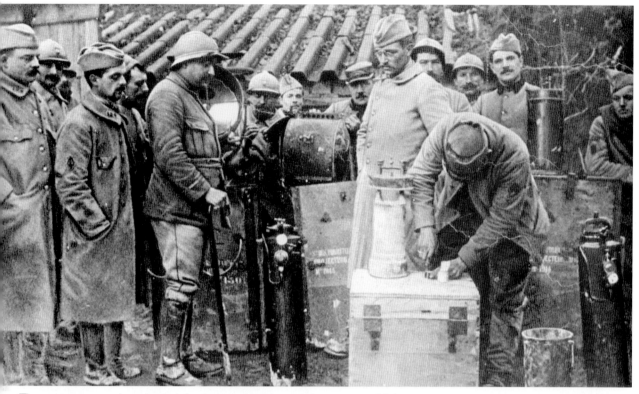

These men are undergoing training in how to set up and use a searchlight.

Annamite troops on the Aisne in a captured German trench. As the trench area is clean, it is almost certain that it is now a rear trench.

Three mountain soldiers in a trench somewhere in the mountains of France; the trench side is being held up with felled trees. The presence of a dog, walking sticks and the general cleanliness suggest it is either a quiet area or the photo was taken some way back from the front. All three are wearing the M1915 horizon blue tunic but in two styles and two are wearing corduroy breeches. The inverted chevrons indicate length of service and the two horizontal bars on the central soldier indicate rank (in this case a lieutenant). They are all wearing a dark blue wool *tarte*, the traditional headwear of the Chasseur battalions.

In the region of the Upper Marne, in the Haut Marne department, across the tract of country lying south and west of Verdun, Metz, Nancy, and the Vosges, the French reserve armies were strongly entrenched. This is a section of the trenches in the Upper Marne, on the outskirts of a village.

The water table in Flanders was very high, so digging a deep trench was almost impossible. The solution was to build trench walls of sand bags. Here the troops are strengthening their defences against flooding.

The most unwanted job was sentry in a forward sap, often very close to the equivalent German position. Note the unusual footwear being worn.

In case of trench raids, 'light-rocket' sentry-posts were established in French trenches at suitable points. Here the rocket sentry is standing ready to light up the ground in front by firing the rocket he is holding, which is lighted automatically. Other rockets were then fired in succession from the magazine in the trench wall.

Fort de la Macédoine was a natural
stronghold consolidated with sand. It was
an Allied fortress in the Balkans.

Both sides used listening posts to
eavesdrop on telephonic communications.
In this photo, two officers in a rocky
dugout are listening to a microphone
through their headphones. Similar
apparatus was used to listen for mining.

This photograph was obviously taken in a very quiet sector, for the officers to be able to enjoy breakfast outdoors with flowers and a tablecloth.

After the morning stand-to many men had time on their hands. During these periods the men would write home.

It was essential to keep the enemy lines under observation at all times in case of a surprise attack. These three men are in the lookout post with one watching through binoculars.

This photograph clearly shows the zig-zag design of French communication trenches. This one is leading to the front in the Champagne region.

Newly arrived from America, General Pershing is passing along a guard of honour, while inspecting it. The men were territorials who were guarding the port.

Before the American entry into the war, a number of Americans had joined the French Army – the Foreign Legion, the aviation corps or as auxiliaries. With America joining the Allied nations, they asked permission to form a separate unit of Americans, bolstered by new arrivals from the United States who could not wait for the draft in their country. Here they are parading and saluting the Stars and Stripes.

These are men of the first American unit: formed as infantry, they wore French steel helmets.

Although eager, the American troops were inexperienced. As with all new troops, they were attached to experienced French regiments to learn the ropes. The three Americans are easily distinguished by their British-style helmet.

(**Above**) French forces were also bolstered by the arrival of thousands of Russian troops. They wore their own uniforms but were equipped from French stocks and trained by French soldiers.

(**Opposite, above**) This photo was taken on 1 August 1916, between Belloy and Estrées, during an attack, with the reserves waiting in a deep trench for the signal to advance.

(**Opposite, below**) To help release French troops for assaults in the east, British troops took over the Arras Front. This picture was taken just before the handover to the British.

This photograph of a lookout could not have been taken on the Western Front: he is far too exposed. This French soldier is looking out for Bulgarians somewhere on the Salonika Front.

A lookout among factory ruins: sentries by the Aisne near Soissons. This outpost was known as the Poste de l'Aquarium, close beside the banks of the Aisne, on the outskirts of St. Vaast, a suburb of the city.

This lookout post is made of sheet-iron plates and strips of canvas on battens, set up in the wrecked basement of a bombarded factory. All about are fallen iron pillars and girders, broken steam pipes, machinery, and rubble.

With the threatened collapse of the Italian Army in 1917, both the French and British sent troops to bolster the front. These are French troops on their way through the Italian countryside to the war zone.

This is first official inspection of the French troops in Italy by General Diaz. To the sound of distant guns, and after the playing of La Marseillaise and the Royal Hymn of Italy, he addressed the men.

French troops resting in a market place somewhere in Venice.

Resting at a newly liberated farm during the 1918 advance.

Like their British allies, the French believed in the value of tanks. This picture shows the detraining of heavy St. Chamond tanks, but where this is, is not known.

With the Germans retreating across relatively undamaged terrain, there was considerable use of light tanks, like these Renault FTs waiting to move forward. This tank was the first to have a fully rotating turret, making it the forerunner of the modern tank.

The temporary office of an Army Corps commander in front of Roye.

As well as their offensive use, they were also useful for bringing back captured German field guns. Here a German 77mm gun is being attached to a heavy tank for taking back.

A trench in the Meuse sector.

This photograph was taken during the Battle of La Malmaison and shows French troops in newly captured positions.

Like their enemy, the French used dogs for scouting, patrol work and to search for the wounded after action. These are *chiens sanitaires* waiting in the trenches before being sent out to locate wounded.

During mobile warfare there was little time or need to build trenches: it became a war of holes, inhabited for the night and left the next day.

Small group advances, reduced casualties and provided smaller targets. This group are in a temporary trench dug in newly re-captured ground.

(**Opposite, above**) Although the Germans were withdrawing, they launched counter-attacks to delay or re-take the positions they vacated. This machine gun team, using a Chauchat, is dug in by the side of the road waiting for an attack.

(**Above**) A St. Chamond heavy tank in action as infantry support.

(**Opposite, below**) Troops waiting for the signal to leave the trenches to continue the attack.

A mobile pigeon coop. When there were no other ways of communicating, the pigeon was almost guaranteed to get through.

This photo shows the first follow-up wave whose responsibility was cleaning up the German trenches.

Here an infantry battalion is studying the ridges they must take during the day. The photo was taken on 30 April 1917.

A Renault FT moving into action. Like British and German tankers, their mounts were named. This is called Marcelle, a gender-neutral name most often given to females.

After a bombardment it was the responsibility of telephone engineers to mend any breaks caused. In this picture the men are wearing gas masks, which would hamper their work but, because the gas did not always dissipate rapidly, it was a wise protection.

This picture was taken during the German Spring Offensive. It shows two machine gunners defending Hangard Wood, south of Villers-Bretonneux (the junction between the French and British Empire forces). The machine gun is the Chauchat.

(**Above**) Following the fall of an enemy position, any captured equipment was taken as trophies. However, sometimes it was more useful to turn it on its previous owners. Here, during an advance, a German machine gun (Maxim, Maschinengewehr 08) is in use by a French machine gun team.

(**Opposite, top**) French infantry leaving their trenches during an offensive.

(**Opposite, middle**) Here the men are leaving their trench under the protection of a creeping barrage.

(**Opposite, bottom**) A rather poor quality image but a very rare one. It shows a line of heavy tanks returning on the night of 16 April 1917, during the fighting between Soissons and Reims.

As the advance developed momentum, the less the towns and countryside showed the signs of fighting. In a newly vacated French town, the men march through accompanied by the Regimental Band.

Not all the newly liberated back-area towns were captured intact. Here cavalry are riding through the result of their own artillery fire.

During the German 1918 offensives, British and French lines sometimes crossed. Here British stretcher bearers are passing through French lines guarded by French machine gunners who are operating an Hotchkiss 8mm machine gun fed by 30-round magazine clips.

German PoWs, under guard, passing through Foucaucourt-en-Santerre.

First-aid posts were set up wherever suitable, often where the enemy had set up theirs. Only days before this photo was taken, this cellar had been a German aid post.

During and after a battle, the work of a First Aid post was constant. Here lightly wounded men wait their turn for medical care.

As previously mentioned, the French used *chiens sanitaires* to find the wounded.

Men from an aid post pose during a quiet time at the front.

In the quiet areas of the Vosges Front, the transport of the wounded was relatively straightforward. Here a wounded man is being placed in a motorcycle sidecar.

In mountainous areas, where everything was covered by trees, it was possible to build up large camps with properly surfaced roads. The motorbike and sidecar is an ambulance; the wounded man is being brought in for treatment.

Here a heavily wounded man is being taken to an ambulance from a hillside aid post.

At a hospital, wounded men from a Moroccan regiment are being presented with bravery awards by Général Dubail and Minister Gaston Doumergue.

As the Germans retreated, it was essential for Allied intelligence to know who they had been fighting against. After the battle moved on, troops were designated to sift through the battle debris to find information.

The German caption for this photograph is simple: 'the wooden cross'.

# Bibliography

Clayton, A. *Paths of Glory. The French Army 1914–18.* Cassell. 2005.

Duroselle, J.B. 'The French Mutinies', in *History of the First World War*, pp. 2133–41. Purnell. 1971.

Jerram, C.S. *The Armies of the World,* Lawrence & Bullen. 1899.

Keegan, J. 'Battle of the Frontiers 1: Lorraine', in *History of the First World War*, pp. 145–9. Purnell. 1969.

Martin, W. *Verdun 1916.* Osprey Publishing. 2001.

Pitt, B. 'Causes of the War', in *History of the First World War*, pp. 20–31. Purnell. 1969.

Porch, D. 'The French Army in the First World War', in *Military Effectiveness*, Vol. 1 (Millet, A.R. & Murray, W. Eds), Cambridge University Press. 2010.

Sumner, I. and Embleton, G. *The French Army 1914–18.* Osprey Military. 1997.

Uffindel, A. *The Nivelle Offensive and the Battle of the Aisne 1917.* Pen & Sword. 2015.

Unknown. *The Marne Battlefields (1914).* Michelin & Cie. 1919.

Unknown. *The Times History of the War, vol. XX.* The Times. 1919.

Unknown. *The Illustrated War News, New Series*, Vols 3–8. The Illustrated London News and Sketch Limited. 1916–1918.

Wilson, H.W. and Hammerton, J.A. *The Great War volume 6.* Amalgamated Press. 1916.

Wilson, H.W. and Hammerton, J.A. *The Great War volume 7.* Amalgamated Press. 1916.

Wilson, H.W. and Hammerton, J.A. *The Great War volume 10.* Amalgamated Press. 1918.

Woodward, D. *Armies of the World 1854–1914.* Sidgwick & Jackson Ltd. 1978.

Young, Brigadier P., DSO, MC. 'Battle of the Frontiers 2: The Ardennes', in *History of the First World War*, pp. 151–5. Purnell. 1969.